Cursing the Darkness

Cursing the Darkness

Destroying the Spirit of Unforgiveness, Bitterness, and Resentment

by John Tetsola

END TIME WAVE
PUBLICATIONS

BOGOTA, NEW JERSEY

Cursing the Darkness
Destroying the Spirit of Unforgiveness, Bitterness, and Resentment

ISBN 0-9634306-6-1

Note: In some Scripture quotations, italics have been added by the author for emphasis only.

Typesetter: Sheila Chang

TABLE OF CONTENTS

DEDICATION

This book is dedicated to you, my son in the Lord and my armorbearer, Perry Mallory, who has continuously worked tirelessly behind the scene to promote and extend the vision that God has given my wife, Vickie, and I. You have been an incredible support to us personally and the ministry that God has given us. I pray that the Lord will reward you for all of your endeavors and that as the Body of Christ reads this powerful book, your labor of love will become a memorial of challenge in their hearts, attest to your good works and provoke men and women, both, to serve their leaders faithfully and unselfishly.

AUTHOR'S PREFACE

One of the most powerful abilities that God has instilled within man is the ability to forgive. Forgiveness is the willingness to master your reactions in the face of an offense. It is always within your power to decide your response to any given situation. You can choose to seethe in the stew of bitterness and resentment, or you can decide to soar above the storms of life. Many people are struggling with the injury and pain of indignities inflicted upon them, whether intentionally or unintentionally. Many have been hurt so deeply and treated so unfairly that it is extremely difficult for them to will to forgive. Yet the facility to forgive still resides within all of us, even in the midst of what may seem like insurmountable pain.

Our freedom and peace in the face of our own guilt depends on the forgiveness that is released from God by His grace and extended towards us. Since none of us has reached the pinnacle of perfection in our daily walk, we are all placed in the same category of needing forgiveness. This then leads us to a vital question....if we have been forgiven by God, dare we fail in exercising forgiveness towards others? We are required to forgive all others who have hurt us, for we must always operate by the universal laws of God which command us to give that we may receive. When we give forgiveness, then we may receive forgiveness. The act of forgiveness identifies us with the Divine nature of Jesus Christ, which is a nature of dominion over all things. We must take dominion over the negative emotions generated in our minds when we are offended or abused, and learn to operate like Christ and absolve those that have despitefully used us.

Unforgiveness possesses the abrasive qualities of the most caustic acid; it will consume and destroy the peace and joy in our soul. Unforgiveness places us under the unnatural spiritual burden of guilt and condemnation, which, as specters, haunt us with a continual litany of accusations against those that have wronged us. We become literally enslaved to their voices, and peace eludes us as we wallow in the quagmire of hate and resentment. Unforgiveness will open the door to many physical problems, such as headaches, ulcers, nervousness and sleeplessness, as well as chronic diseases such as arthritis. Bitterness, anger and resentment will literally sink into our bones if we do not rid ourselves of these attitudes. Unforgiveness becomes a blockade in the pathway to our blessings, and, unless subdued, will torment us by creating a hellish dissatisfaction with life through our unrighteous judgement of others. When this happens, we are placed into a perpetual state of anger, and, since we were not designed to function within that emotion for long periods of time, our brains react to the negativity by emitting certain chemicals that are detrimental to our health and well-being. It is almost as if our bodies have a law within their members that, when violated, will issue a command to self-destruct. The symptoms experienced through UNFORGIVENESS are not worth the toll they take on our body.

John Tetsola
June 1996

CHAPTER ONE

MY PERSONAL WOUND

Who said, The Lord really is risen, and has appeared to Simon [Peter]!

Then they [themselves] related in full what had happened on the road, and how He was known *and* recognized by them in the breaking of bread.

Now while they were talking about this, Jesus Himself took His stand among them and said to them, Peace [that is, freedom from all the distresses that are experienced as the result of sin] be to you!

But they were so startled and terrified that they thought they saw a spirit.

And He said to them, Why are you disturbed *and* troubled, and why do such doubts *and* questionings arise in your hearts?

See my hands and My feet, that it is I Myself; feel of *and* handle Me and see, for a spirit does not have flesh and bones as you see that I have.

And when He had said this, He showed them His hands and His feet.

Luke 24:34-40 (AMP)

These Scriptures record the turning point for the Church in its history. This was the occurrence when Jesus had returned and appeared to some of the disciples. He had now been resurrected. The Bible tells us here that when Jesus stood in their midst (verse 37), the disciples became startled, troubled. Many times one's real presence, state, condition or status can looked upon as being unbelievable, go unnoticed or even challenged. The revealing of this truth can many times startle us. Just as Jesus, Himself, was now being mistaken for a spirit, so too are mistaken identities common at this stage of evaluating one's position or condition.

As numerous doubts and questionings arose in the hearts of the disciples, Jesus released an unprecedented principle. Jesus said, "See My hands and My feet." Not only was He telling them to witness His physical scars, but also He was exposing His inflicted wounds. Exposing your wounds is beneficial to all involved. It allows inner healing as you share your own wounds and also it helps those listening and witnessing your testimony.

Internal

The next incredible principle that Jesus laid down was when He told them to "feel of and handle me." Jesus was saying, "Not only witness my wounds, come on, experience my wounds; feel my wounds; feel what I feel." Jesus wanted His experience to be experienced by the disciples for an understanding. Jesus wasn't asking the disciples to go through what He went through, but to allow His experience to be their own experience.

I have found great relief and power in exposing my personal wounds. Exposure permits those around you to "experience" how real you actually are. Exposing your wounds also will destroy the hidden spirits of unforgiveness, bitterness and resentment.

A few years ago, the Spirit of the Lord began to deal with my heart concerning the spirit of UNFORGIVENESS. My wife and I were under a ministry that really hurt and disappointed us. The leadership of the ministry and some of his associates would get on the pulpit and begin to preach unjustifiable accusations against us. My wife would leave the church crying after every service. It came to the point that almost every member of the church knew who the leadership or the associates were talking about. It became a message of attack. Then they applied the isolation strategy, where almost everyone felt uncomfortable talking to us because of how the leadership of the house would react and what would be said to them. Some of the folks were directly instructed not to have anything to do with us, and those who dared to relate to us endured repeated rebuke or eventually learned to isolate themselves. Other people could afford to be comfortable with us outside the environment of the church, but not within the walls of the church. We later found out that it was the same strategy and tactic that was used by the leadership on others who used to be a part of the ministry. I began to develop a strong spirit of bitterness and resentment towards this individual and his ministry. His behavior really angered, upset and hurt my heart, for it was unjustified and I assessed his behavior as unbecoming for one who was walking with God. I could tolerate his rejection and ridicule if it only concerned myself. But my wife was involved. Her integrity was being smeared, also. She was emotionally crushed. She never looked forward to the services because she knew the antagonistic lecture that the leader would spew from the pulpit. I had to encourage her to come along with me to church. We were both walking with more than our share of anger and bitterness. Our pain had become a familiar friend....we embraced our agony and justified our injurious sentiments. And when we finally left the ministry, I was so hurt that I made up my mind not to speak to or have any dealings with the leadership and that particular ministry ever again.

It was in this season and time that the Spirit of the Lord began to deal with our hurt. He began to whisper strongly about the need to forgive and urged us to allow Him to destroy the root of unforgiveness, bitterness and resentment which had taken residence within us. Today, we are able to face and talk with these individuals without unforgiveness, bitterness or any form of resentment lodged in our hearts. The reason for this is an encounter I had with the Spirit of the Lord while I was on my knees praying. He spoke very strongly to my heart and said, "Son, let it drop." Then I said, "Lord, let what drop?" Then the Lord said "Son, let that hurt, resentment and bitterness go." The very moment I agreed with the Lord to let it drop, there was a strong surge of the anointing that came all over me from the crown of my head to the soles of my feet! I could perceive that those contrary and evil spirits had been broken over my life. I felt a strong love rising up inside of me towards this leader and his ministry. This love has always been there. It was there before he offended me. But it was being obstructed by unforgiveness, bitterness and resentment. After this phenomenal experience in prayer, I picked up the phone and called him. I wanted to just verbalize how much I loved him and tell of the respect that I have for his ministry. I was a changed man! The flow of love and compassion was unhindered. Even though I could still see the flaws in him and in his ministry, there was a genuine, supernatural love which I can not explain that was aimed toward him and his work. This love was intense enough to cover his flaws. I love him and appreciate him so much more than he may never, ever know, even now!

I am believing, through your reading of this book, that the Spirit of God will cause deliverance to come to you in whatever area of hurt, disappointment, bitterness and resentment that you are experiencing, for like me, you need to let go, and let God!

CHAPTER TWO

THE DANGER OF UNFORGIVENESS

And do not grieve the Holy Spirit of God, (do not offend, or vex, or sadden Him) by Whom you were sealed (marked, branded as God's own, secured) for the day of redemption - of final deliverance through Christ from evil and the consequences of sin.

Let all bitterness and indignation and wrath (passion, rage, bad temper) and resentment (anger, animosity) and quarreling (brawling, clamor, contention) and slander (evilspeaking, abusive or blasphemous language) be banished from you, with all malice (spite, ill will or baseness of any kind).

And become useful and helpful and kind to one another, tenderhearted (compassionate, understanding, loving-hearted), forgiving one another [readily and freely], as God in Christ forgave you.

Ephesians 4:30-32(Amp)

For thou, Lord, *art* good, and ready to forgive; and plenteous in mercy unto all them that call upon thee.

Psalms 86:5

And forgive us our debts, as we forgive our debtors.

And lead us not into temptation, but deliver us from evil: For thine is the kingdom, and the power, and the glory, for ever. Amen.

For if ye forgive men their trespasses, your heavenly Father will also forgive you:

But if ye forgive not men their trespasses, neither will your Father forgive your trespasses.

Matthew 6:12-15

Most of us do not really understand the power of forgiveness that we possess. Nor do we really understand the effects of the power of unforgiveness that will work against us. This power is so lethal that it can be compared to electricity. If the current is flowing properly, electricity enhances our existence and enables us to enjoy a measure of luxury in our daily lives. Yet if we violate the laws governing electricity, and stick our wet fingers in an open socket, we'll experience a backlash of power that brings a burning destruction that will consume us. This is why it is so vital that we understand the power of forgiveness.

To forgive means to "excuse a fault and to pardon an offense." When someone is in prison and the governor pardons them, he is giving them something they don't really deserve. In other words, they did something that deserves punishment, but he has decided to exercise his authority and ability to judge the matter and pardon the offender. The governor releases them into freedom and liberty from the bondage of their offensive action even when they deserve to be punished.

That's the most remarkable thing about forgiveness; no one ever deserves to be forgiven-- EVER!! Forgiveness is something that is chosen to be given because forgiveness is an expression of the nature of God. We were made in His Image. We stand as His ambassadors and His representatives in this earth. He first forgave us when we offended Him, and He expects us to sow and plant the seeds of forgiveness into the lives of others that may offend us. As we do this, then we place ourselves in position to receive the blessing of continual forgiveness for all of our sins throughout all of our relationship with God.

Forgiveness also carries an additional definition: "to absolve from payment". In other words, we need to be freed of the "tit for tat" syndrome! Some people spend most of their lives trying to make somebody pay them back for some transgression against the essence of their being, which is an exercise in futility. You can never take vengeance into your own hands. You lack the wisdom, skill and strategy to do it effectively. God did not instill the ability to effect retribution within us. This is why He states that "Vengeance is Mine and I will repay." Vengeance requires expertise. Why not allow the Expert to handle these issues of life?

Then came Peter to him, and said, Lord, how oft shall my brother sin against me, and I forgive him? till seven times?

Jesus saith unto him, I say not unto thee, Until seven times: but, Until seventy times seven.

Matthew 18:21-22

The Vines Dictionary gives further definitions of forgiveness: "to send away, to forgive a debt, to completely cancel, and the remission of all punishment due." Sometimes we say that we forgive people and we punish them anyway. You say you forgive them but you won't talk to them. You say you forgive them but yet you give them the cold shoulder. You say you forgive them and yet you talk ugly about them behind their backs. You see, true forgiveness means the remission of all the punishment that they deserve. If you are going to forgive somebody, then you cannot punish them any longer.

Forgiveness also means to unconditionally bestow a favor. Forgiveness is given with no conditional strings attached. You don't have to love your enemy to forgive him. He does not have to be saved for you to forgive him. He does not have to be white or black for you to forgive him. He does not have to be your friend to forgive him. You have the ability to forgive regardless of the attributes of his character.

Forgiveness also means "to let loose." "to release" or "to let go of". The implication is to let the issue drop and to leave it. This is exactly what God did for us. The Amplified Bible says to forgive means "TO JUST DROP IT." Sometimes a person may do something to us, and instead of dropping it, we just continue to talk about it and fan the flames of contention instead of just dropping it. Yet every fire will burn itself out if its hunger for fuel is denied.

"FOR" VERSUS "GIVE"

For God so loved the world, that he gave his only begotten Son, that whosoever believeth in him should not perish, but have everlasting life.

John 3:16

Let us divide the word "forgive" in half and you will find some very interesting truths within these two words. Let's examine the first word, "FOR." The word "FOR" is a word that is used to indicate the purpose of an activity. In other words, if a car is sitting in a car lot or dealership, that car is "FOR" sale. If a dress, a shirt or a suit is in a department store, they are considered "FOR" sale. The word "GIVE" means "to make a present offer," "to convey an offer" or "to denote or provide free of charge." Therefore, what we are really doing when we forgive someone is that we are simply making a free donation to them with no strings attached. You are simply giving them an offering of grace.

We must be willing to accept God's will which is to forgive as we have been forgiven. It is not a matter of who is right or who is wrong. Forgiveness transcends your judgement in the matter, for the will of God is the principle thing. We must choose to forgive, and be willing to obey God. If we are willing, God is able to give us the grace to forgive. But when we do forgive, we must forgive unconditionally! So often we'll say "Well, I will forgive if she or he apologizes first." This is conditional forgiveness that only touches the surface of tho matter. The heart has not forgiven, and

11

the blackness of the embers of resentment are still smoldering. Other times we are silent towards a person, but in actuality, we are really punishing them with our silence. We are shouting inwardly, "This is the price you must pay for my forgiveness" as our exterior face attempts to mask our evil intentions. Jesus' forgiveness is extended towards us without any strings attached and ours must be the same.

WHY WE MUST FORGIVE

And grieve not the holy Spirit of God, whereby ye are sealed unto the day of redemption.

Let all bitterness, and wrath, and anger, and clamour, and evil speaking, be put away from you, with all malice:

And be ye kind one to another, tenderhearted, forgiving one another, even as God for Christ's sake hath forgiven you.

Ephesians 4:30-32

The primary reason why we need to forgive is simply because God said to. God demands obedience. Really, if we don't have any other reason why we need to forgive, then His commandment should be sufficient. We should do it simply because God said to do it. You can do something and reap the benefit of it even if you don't totally understand why God is asking you to do it. We can save ourselves lots of trouble while on this earth if we just read the Bible and do what it says. Sometimes we don't have to know all the "why's" before we do a thing. Just do it. When we refuse to obey God, then we move into an arena of disobedience, and all disobedience will reap its just rewards.

YOUR FAITH WON'T WORK

And saith unto them, Go your way into the village over against you: and as soon as ye be entered into it, ye shall find a colt tied, whereon never man sat; loose him, and bring *him.*

And if any man say unto you, Why do ye this? say ye that the Lord hath need of him; and straightway he will send him hither.

And they went their way, and found the colt tied by the door without in a place where two ways met; and they loose him.

And certain of them that stood there said unto them, What do ye, loosing the colt?

And they said unto them even as Jesus had commanded: and they let them go.

And they brought the colt to Jesus, and cast their garments on him; and he sat upon him.

And many spread their garments in the way: and others cut down branches off the trees, and strowed *them* in the way.

And they that went before, and they that followed, cried, saying, Hosanna; Blessed *is* he that cometh in the name of the Lord:

Blessed *be* the kingdom of our father David, that cometh in the name of the Lord: Hosanna in the highest.

And Jesus entered into Jerusalem, and into the temple: and when he had looked round about upon all things, and now the eventide was come, he went out unto Bethany with the twelve.

And on the morrow, when they were come from Bethany, he was hungry:

And seeing a fig tree afar off having leaves, he came, if haply he might find any thing thereon: and when he came to it, he found nothing but leaves; for the time of figs was not *yet.*

And Jesus answered and said unto it, No man eat fruit of thee hereafter for ever. And his disciples heard *it.*

And they come to Jerusalem: and Jesus went into the temple, and began to cast out them that sold and bought in the temple, and overthrew the tables of the moneychangers, and the seats of them that sold doves;

And would not suffer that any man should carry *any* vessel through the temple.

And he taught, saying unto them, Is it not written, My house shall be called of all nations the house of prayer? but ye have made it a den of thieves.

And the scribes and chief priests heard *it,* and sought how they might destroy him: for they feared him, because all the people was astonished at his doctrine.

And when even was come, he went out of the city.

And in the morning, as they passed by, they saw the fig tree dried up from the roots.

And Peter calling to remembrance saith unto him, Master, behold, the fig tree which thou cursedst is withered away.

And Jesus answering saith unto them, Have faith in God.

For verily I say unto you, That whosoever shall say unto this mountain, Be thou removed, and be thou cast into the sea; and shall not doubt in his heart, but shall believe that those things which he saith shall come to pass; he shall have whatsoever he saith.

Therefore I say unto you, What things soever ye desire, when ye pray, believe that ye receive *them,* and ye shall have *them.*

And when ye stand praying, forgive, if ye have ought against any: that your Father also which is in heaven may forgive you your trespasses. -

But if ye do not forgive, neither will your Father which is in heaven forgive your trespasses.

And they come again to Jerusalem: and as he was walking in the temple, there come to him the chief priests, and the scribes, and the elders,

Mark 11: 2-27

But without faith *it is* impossible to please *him:* for he that cometh to God must believe that he is, and *that* he is a rewarder of them that diligently seek him.

Hebrews 11:6

Above all, taking the shield of faith, wherewith ye shall be able to quench all the fiery darts of the wicked.

Ephesians 6:16

Your faith won't work if you don't forgive. This is very important, because you need faith in everything you do. The Bible says that without faith, it is impossible to please God. If you cannot please God then you cannot receive from Him. You can never receive from anyone that you cannot afford to please. What God is simply saying is that there is no other route to receive from Him, if it is not through the route of faith. We are supposed to live in faith; we are faith people. Everything we receive from God is received through the channel of faith. No matter what God is trying to give us; if we don't have our faith working, we are not going to receive it and we are not going to believe it.

Your faith won't work as long as you harbor unforgiveness and bitterness in your heart. In Ephesians 6, we are commanded to put on the whole armor of God. Above all, we are encouraged to utilize the shield of faith with which we quench all the fiery darts of the enemy. The little offenses that we entertain are a trap from the devil to lead us into the next step which is a progressive trip into bitterness, resentment and eventually, a dangerous case of full blown unforgiveness to block our faith and disturb our relationship with God.

We can be harboring unforgiveness because we have not dealt with something somebody has done to us. Sometimes, we're unaware that it is lodged in our hearts and we walk around like everything is alright. We must learn to treat unforgiveness like a plague. Let's learn to be quick to forgive and keep ourselves clean from the taint of unforgiveness. Sometimes we offer excuses by saying, "Yeah, but you don't know what they did to me," or "Yeah, but you don't know how bad they hurt me." In God's program, there is no "Yeah, but....." You need to understand that God is not trying to be mean, but He is trying to send blessings to us. And He is trying to show us that He cannot send them to us if we don't operate according to the laws of His program. Bitterness, resentment and unforgiveness are of the devil's program. These not of God's program.

HARD TIMES

At my first trial no one acted in my defense (as my advocate) or took my part or [even] stood with me, but all forsook me. May it not be charged against them!

II Timothy 4:16 (Amp)

Sometimes we are confronted by hard things that are unfair and difficult to understand. But even in the midst, we still have to always keep the principle of forgiving people foremost in our heart. We must always be ready to let go of all those offenses, because there is no way God can straighten out our problems if we don't stay on His program of forgiveness. The devil wants our pipes to be blocked up.

UNFORGIVENESS PRODUCES FILTHINESS IN YOUR INNER MAN

Wherefore, my beloved brethren, let every man be swift to hear, slow to speak, slow to wrath:

For the wrath of man worketh not the righteousness of God.

Wherefore lay apart all filthiness and superfluity of naughtiness, and receive with meekness the engrafted word, which is able to save your souls.

But be ye doers of the word, and not hearers only, deceiving your own selves.

For if any be a hearer of the word, and not a doer, he is like unto a man beholding his natural face in a glass:

For he beholdeth himself, and goeth his way, and straightway forgetteth what manner of man he was.

But whoso looketh into the perfect law of liberty, and continueth *therein,* he being not a forgetful hearer, but a doer of the work, this man shall be blessed in his deed.

James 1:19-25

Another important reason why you must forgive, is because unforgiveness leads to dirt accumulation in the inner man. Unforgiveness is not the only thing that leads to spiritual filthiness. There are also other things. But unforgiveness is just one of them. The Bible says that we need to be washed in the water of the Word. You don't need to be washed if you are not dirty. Only dirty people need to be washed. It is not our outer body that gets washed by the Word. It is our inner man. The Word, when spoken, bypasses your body and it literally goes inside of you, affecting anything and everything that stands in its way. And when the entire service is over, you have literally taken a bath with the detergent of the Word. This is kind of helpful because when you know that somebody hurt you and you are bitter and resentful towards them, you can always run to the bathroom of the Word and take a good bath to wash out the filthiness that the bitterness, resentment and unforgiveness has left in you. The quicker you forgive someone that hurts you, the easier it is. The longer you wait, the more you think about it. Every time you refuse to forgive for a minute, the root of the monster gets a little deeper in your soul.

THE TORTURE OF UNFORGIVENESS

Unforgiveness, bitterness and resentment produces torture in our own lives. The question is, what smart person would torture themselves? We always want God to forgive us, but we are not often ready to give unto other people what God has given to us. When we have the junk of bitterness, resentment and unforgiveness in us, it tortures us. Many times we want to hold onto the unforgiveness, but we are not ready to pay the price of the torture, torment, discomfort, and even physical sickness that comes along with it. But you will always pay the price for it if you keep it. Yet, you only pay the price for it if you hang on to it. You are not hurting the other person through the nurturing of your anger, like you think. You are literally hurting yourself.

You have already been hurt by what was said or what was done. But the devil likes you to hold on to the hurt and resentment because he uses it to keep a perpetual litany of pain echoing in your ears. Every time you see, hear or talk to the person, you are still hurt. Don't you know that if you have unforgiveness against someone, that your heart will ache the moment you lay your eyes upon them? Everytime someone mentions their name, you hurt. Not the other person, but you. You are continually being wounded afresh. No matter what someone has done to you, you have been hurt enough! Don't let it keep hurting you! It never stops hurting you until you let it go. Most of the ground that satan gains is through unforgiveness.

I believe that when we harbor unforgiveness, bitterness and resentment, we are tortured by a number of things. The first torture produced is depression. The reason depression is produced is because unforgiveness, bitterness and resentment put a heaviness on your spirit. Your joy departs. You're just not happy. You cannot be happy and carry that load of unforgiveness, resentment or bitterness with you. It will betray you.

You may try to be happy when the person who offended you is not around you, but whenever they are in your midst, the heaviness reappears. With some Christians, they begin to develop flashes of something that was done to them; all because they did not forgive and let it drop. Understand this, your debt will be paid. But you cannot pay it. You don't do the paying. God does the paying.

As a result of not dealing with these spirits, you then are tortured by the spirit of jealousy and envy. You are also assaulted by the spirit of anger. You get angry over every little thing that the perpertrators do. Finally, the spirit of hatred comes to add insult to your injury. This spirit will compel you to bad mouth every single thing they try to do. And your inner anger has found a release that exposes the hatred building within your temple.

THE BLOCKING OF YOUR RELATIONSHIP WITH GOD

For if ye forgive men their trespasses, your heavenly Father will also forgive you:

But if ye forgive not men their trespasses, neither will your Father forgive your trespasses.

Matthew 6:14-15

Unforgiveness will block your personal relationship with God. It will hinder your ability to enjoy the manifested Presence of God. If you sense that you have difficulty in entering God's Presence, you should examine your life to see if you are harboring a grudge or if you are moving in a realm of unforgiveness. That does not have to be the only reason, but that may be one of the major reasons. As soon as there is unforgiven sin between you and God, it automatically blocks your personal relationship with Him. It deadens your ability to enjoy the sensing of the Presence of God when you go to spend time with Him.

BITTERNESS CANNOT PRODUCE LOVE

The reason you have to forgive is because you cannot love without it. Let me give you an example. Maybe you had a miserable marriage or familial relationship. Perhaps you were hurt really bad and one of you left and some years after that, God decides to bless you with someone else that will treat you correctly. You will not be able to love the new person properly if you have not totally forgiven the other person that hurt you. You'll continue to carry the imagery of your pain into the new relationship. It is important that you get rid of that bitterness, resentment and spiritual filthiness. Even in a good marriage, until one is able to forgive the other of something that was done wrong, both of the partners cannot love one another properly. Unforgiveness is equivalent to hatred. You cannot love and hate at the same time.

YOU OPENED THE DOOR!

If you forgive any one anything, I too forgive that one; and what I have forgiven, if I have forgiven anything, has been for your sakes in the presence [and with the approval] of Christ, the Messiah,

To keep Satan from getting the advantage over us; for we are not ignorant of his wiles *and* intentions.

II Corinthians 2:10-11 (Amp)

When angry, do not sin; do not ever let your wrath - your exasperation, your fury or indignation - last until the sun goes down.

Leave no [such] room or foothold for the devil - give no opportunity to him.

Ephesians 4:26-27 (Amp)

Unforgiveness, bitterness and resentment opens up a big door for the devil in your own life. If you realize that there is an enemy standing on your front porch, you ought to be smart enough not to open your door to him. You need to remember that the enemy is always hanging around us, waiting for an opportunity to foster defeat in our lives. We often forget to remain alert and keep satan from having the advantage over us. It is not about who is right or wrong or who deserves it or not. It is about preventing an open door for the enemy to show up.

Anger is an emotion that God gave to us to let us know when somebody is mistreating us. Don't feel guilty that you sense the feeling of anger rising up in you from time to time. But when the feeling begins to rise up in you, quench the thirst of that feeling with the Word of God.

The Bible says that when you feel angry, do not sin. In other words, re-channel your anger to something else. Go to the Word of God or pray concerning the matter and then let it drop. Resist the enemy of anger or give an offering of forgiveness. Look at what verse 27 says. It says "leave no foot hold for the devil." A foothold is a base of operation in your life that allows the enemy to advance. It is a springboard or a legitimate excuse that the enemy can present before God to be allowed into any area of your life that he wills to enter. God Himself cannot stop him. The devil and his spirits automatically have a right to a passage into your life as a result of the foothold that you give him.

The devil is concerned about the CENTER PLACE of our lives that is occupied by God. He desires to block our communication with God so that we cannot hear and pray effectively. His strategy is to discourage us so that our faith won't work. But the devil cannot occupy this center place unless we give him a foothold or a permission slip. Staying angry and harboring offenses is a foothold that the devil needs to progress to the next place that he wants to occupy in our lives.

Let me say this: when you feel offended, don't always assume immediately that it is the other person offending you. There may be something bothering you that makes you take an offense over what you have no business being offended about. The Bible says that we are not to be "touchy." Love is not "touchy." "Touchiness" stems from repetitive offenses that create a premise of unforgiving thoughts and formulate one's bitter attitudes towards life. A lot of people get offended when you just look at them, because even then, a look becomes an offensive threat.

To offend someone means "to displease," "to affront" and "to anger." What causes this deep anger that we are not suppose to sleep on? Sometimes, its just a series of little things -- somebody cuts you off on the highway, or pushes their shopping cart ahead of you in the grocery line, or interrupts you or accuses you of what you did not do, and on and on it goes! Opportunities present themselves daily for us to become offended. When we cling to the notion that we must defend our "rights" in a matter, then we will continually become offended. Someone will always trespass on the boundaries of how we feel we should be treated. Someone will always bring an irritation. But the greater power is within you....the ability to forgive.

He who covers *and* forgives an offense seeks love, but he who repeats *or* harps on a matter separates even close friends.

Proverbs 17:9 (Amp)

The Bible admonishes us to *cover* offenses. In other words, if we want to be lovers of God and want to walk in the love of God, then we have to be prepared everyday -- all day long to cover offenses. How do we cover offenses? By constantly forgiving and letting it drop. When somebody offends you, one of the ways you can cover their offense is to agree with God that you are not going to tell anybody else about it.

I encourage you to do this. If you are in a place and somebody offends you, you need to open your mouth and say these words "Father God, I forgive them and I let it drop." Continue to say it until your spirit man begins to agree with you and accepts it.

The Greek word for "offense" is **"SKANDALON"**. The word "skandalon" was originally the name of a part of a trap on which bait was attached. Offenses that come on us or against us all

25

day long are the devil's bait. What the devil tries to do, is to make you take his bait so that he can trap you on his hook! But don't bite the bait!!

He wants you to soak that thing up, meditate on it, roll it over on the inside of you and get two or three more on top of each and roll it over and over again and then think about it some more. Then there is an attempt to get you into a little of bitterness and then into resentment and then you are now progressing into full blown unforgiveness. Now you cannot pray, and you cannot fellowship with God. You cannot do anything except sit around and wonder what is wrong with you. The bait is the devil's device. When you are in a situation that produces unforgiveness, you have to be careful of the devil's bait. Not every bait catches every fish, since every fish is different and may respond with a different appetite. Christians are also different. Their temperaments vary and the bait that the devil may use for one might be quite different from the bait used for another.

The devil produces bait through our thoughts. He makes us think, meditate and ponder on hurts or on what somebody said, how somebody acted, how they greeted us or how they responded when you greeted them. If you're bitter about something, you will misinterpret the actions of people and become offended AGAIN. The devil enjoys making you see things that aren't there. He loves deception. And he especially loves watching you react to what is actually nothing. He can only use this strategy on those who are still prone to react, for they haven't mastered the ability to respond in wisdom.

CHAPTER THREE

HOLDING THE GRUDGE

A grudge is simply an ill will. It's a resentment that is singed in the fires of bitterness. This is one of the most subtle spirits that will latch itself onto you unawares. Often it is the full blown things that we notice, like the full blown anger, temper or wrath. But we fail to notice the small things. But these big problems actually stem from very small problems. Sometimes we have the little offenses and the little grudges stored up on the inside of us towards people and they are really good at hiding. They have not become big monsters yet. Grudges would be equal to an offense. The devil continually works at trying to bring offenses between people, because he knows that the bait that he uses will drag them into a greater problem of hatred.

Grudges need disguises to appear quite small and harmless. First they come looking like sweet, little baby problems -- no big deal. A grudge wants to belong to you. He wants you to hug him.

The first principle to understand is that grudges are baby attitudes. They like to be nursed and like to be held. There is a common expression, "Are you holding a grudge?" The devil will come and offer you a grudge. Every time an offense comes, the devil will always want to offer you a grudge to hold. If you take the grudge or hold the grudge, the next thing the devil will want you to do is to nurse the grudge.

And the second time the cock crew. And Peter called to mind the word that Jesus said unto him, Before the cock crow twice, thou shalt deny me thrice. And when he thought thereon, he wept.

Mark 14:72

The LORD of hosts hath sworn, saying, Surely as I have thought, so shall it come to pass; and as I have purposed, *so* shall it stand:

Isaiah 14:24

O Jerusalem, wash thine heart from wickedness, that thou mayest be saved. How long shall thy vain thoughts lodge within thee?

Jeremiah 4:14

What is the formula for your grudge? Simply, feasting on the thoughts of what has been done to you. Every time an offense comes and you hang on to that offense, it becomes a grudge. And right behind that grudge will come negative thoughts about the person that is going to feed that grudge if you don't get rid of it while you can. Grudges like to be held.

I hate *vain* thoughts: but thy law do I love.

Psalms 119:113

The first thing to do is to develop an hatred for vain thoughts. You must develop a passion to hate thoughts that are not in line with the Word.

How precious also are thy thoughts unto me, O God! how great is the sum of them!

Psalms 139:17

The next thing to do is to cherish and embrace God's thoughts. Make up your mind not to feast on offenses and grudges. Instead, feast on God's thoughts.

The way to avoid holding a grudge is to understand that grudges like people who don't forgive quickly. The key word here is QUICKLY. It is not enough just to forgive, but we must do so quickly. The quicker we forgive, the easier it is to do it. We need to practice quick forgiveness. You see, the negative thought will sit on a bench close to the grudge ready to feed him. The thought will present the picture constantly to grudge. You can always recognize a grudge by their complaining about other people. Grudges must have angry and hateful thoughts to make them grow. When we are quick to forgive, the negative thought cannot penetrate our minds. It is paralyzed, and will have no entry into our lives.

GRUDGES CRAVE FOR AGREEMENT TO SURVIVE

A grudge needs you to agree with it. So it attempts to convince and persuade you to stay in agreement with it. The grudge knows that it alone cannot get the job done. You can tell when the grudge is speaking, when it is attempting to persuade you into agreement. It'll say "I will never forget what he or she did to me and I will never let her forget it either,"

Grudges come by us taking those thoughts unto ourselves and meditating upon them. And as we begin to feed it, it begins to get bigger and bigger. When a grudge is small, you can pick it up and put it down. Keep in mind that if you don't keep it down and leave it down, it is going to keep growing. Anger is one of the things that feeds grudges. If you keep that anger, it will grow and get larger. Don't hug a grudge. Say no to it. Grudges grow up to be resentment, and you cannot hold resentment. Resentment doesn't sit on your lap like a baby. Resentment is like a towering dinosaur; resentment will hold you. Resentment always wants to get even. It makes you unfriendly to those that you should love.

THE PRESSURES OF BITTERNESS

Then, when bitterness is seeded in you, the root goes down before the problem shows up. A lot of times, before you recognize that you have a problem, that thing is already intertwined in your personality to the point that you now need serious ministering to get rid of it. Bitterness squeezes your mind and makes you sick with hateful thoughts. This is how the squeezing is done. "I will not talk to her," "I will just sit down and do nothing," "I don't care what he says, I will do what I want", "I will get her back," "I will not loan her any money when she asks me," etc. Bitterness squeezes every amount of sweetness you have. Warning, it takes humility to forgive somebody that does not deserve it.

What the devil wants you to do when you are offended is to build walls around yourself. The devil wants you to build many walls and keep everybody else out and think that you are protecting yourself by keeping yourself behind these walls of protection. The Bible talks a lot about walls. There are right walls that need to be built in our lives and God says He will build them. But what the devil wants is for us to build unnecessary walls that will isolate us from nurturing relationships. God uses His Word to tear down the wrong walls in our lives so that He can build up the right walls.

Every offense that you entertain can be compared to a brick. The devil wants to provide you with enough bricks so that you can keep yourself walled in real good. Bitterness and resentment are like the mortar that holds the bricks together. You are the bricklayer. You must decide what you are going to do with every brick the devil gives to you. You must decide if you are going to give it back to him or if you will throw it away and refuse to use it. Then you will never have those wrong walls built around your life.

TWO-FOLD RESPONSIBILITY OF OFFENSE

There is a two-fold responsibility that comes whenever offense appears. The first responsibility is that we don't take offense. The devil is going to try to give it to you, but you don't have to take it.

When they were going about here and there in Galilee, Jesus said to them, The Son of man is going to be turned over to the hands of men.

And they will kill Him, and He will rise [to life] again on the third day. And they were deeply *and* exceedingly grieved and distressed.

When they arrived in Capernaum, the collectors of the half-shekel [the temple tax] went up to Peter and said, Does not your Teacher pay the half-shekel?

He answered, Yes. And when he came home, Jesus spoke to him [about it] first, saying, What do you think, Simon? From whom do earthly rulers collect duties or tribute? from their own family - Jesus said to him, Then the sons are exempt.

However, in order not to give offense and cause them to stumble - that is, to judge unfavorably and unjustly - go down to the sea and throw in a hook; take the first fish that comes up, and when you open its mouth you will find there a shekel. Take it and give it to them to pay the temple tax for Me and for yourself.

Matthew 17:22-27 (Amp)

I know and am convinced (persuaded) as one in the Lord Jesus, that nothing is [forbidden as] essentially unclean - that is, defiled and unholy in itself. But [none the less] it is unclean (defiled and unholy) to any one who thinks it is unclean.

But if your brother is being pained or his feelings hurt or if he is being injured by what you eat, [then] you are no longer walking in love. -That is, you have ceased to be living and conducting yourself by the standard of love toward him. Do not let what you eat hurt or cause the ruin of one for whom Christ died!

Do not therefore let what seems good to you be considered an evil thing [by someone else]. - [In other words], do not give occasion for others to criticize that which is justifiable for you.

Romans 14:14-16 (Amp)

The second responsibility is that you don't offend other people. We must determine that we will not purposely offend others. Do everything in your power to avoid offending people.

CHAPTER FOUR

THE "BENEFIT OF THE DOUBT" PRINCIPLE

The "benefit of the doubt" principle is a common principle that we often mention and practice daily in our lives. Yet we don't always take it very seriously. We must understand that this is a very strong principle of deliverance. The Church needs to start taking this principle more seriously than we have been doing. It may sound simple, but is a key tool of deliverance. We often hear people say "Give him the benefit of the doubt; it is not his fault," "Give her the benefit of the doubt; she is just new in the city," "Give him the benefit of the doubt; he just woke up from sleep," or "Give him the benefit of the doubt; he had a bad headache."

Even the judicial system seems to understand and practice this principle more than the Body of Christ. When an individual commits a crime, often attorneys like to use insanity as a defense. What they are simply doing is transferring the blame from their client to some other circumstances which they claim is responsible for their client's actions. Often we get upset when the judge sets those individuals free. We always want the individuals to pay for their crime. That may sound correct, especially if you or your relative or friend are the ones that the crime was committed against. But the truth of the matter is that there is a strong and powerful principle being utilized. If it were thoroughly understood, we would be released from the very pang of bitterness, hurt and resentment that most of us have been living in for years. Like the judge in the court of law, our Chief Judge is willing to release us, to destroy and to set us free from any unforgiveness if we, the victims, would take the "benefit of the doubt" position for our enemies or for those who have hurt us.

Our perspective in matters should be just like that of the attorneys of the court, who are simply pleading before the judge not to blame the individual for the crime. They are attempting to cause the judge to focus the blame on something else that has caused the individual to commit the crime. Many times attorneys argue that child abuse, sexual abuse, and mental problems caused the individual to do what they did. Interesting enough, Jesus practiced this simple but awesome principle. The "benefit of the doubt" principle will prevent the spirit of hurt, bitterness and resentment from taking root in you.

Understanding this principle and operating in it will do the following:

1) It will prevent you from dwelling or building your tent in the arena of hurt and disappointment.

We are called to live in heavenly places in Christ Jesus. We're not to abide in the desert of resentment and bitterness when things don't go the way we think they should have. The desert place is a waste place. It is an utter waste to dwell in unforgiveness.

2) It will help you avoid the spirit of revenge and retaliation. You may desire to analyze the

reasons why you're hurt and then begin to strategize your revenge; how you are not going to talk to them again or how you are going to avoid them or snub them. But when you make up your mind to operate in the principles of God, you will never have to stay in the arena of hurt and bitterness for a long time.

3) It will create an access, a roadway or an opportunity for you to understand the operation of an individual. Many times when we are in bitterness, it is never easy to really understand and learn why a person did what they did. All we are interested in is our own pain and the consuming desire for revenge. But it will help us at this very point of hurt or disappointment to take one step back and begin to understand the operation of that individual and then allow this principle of the "benefit of the doubt" to be unleashed within us.

Operating in this principle, will produce the spirit of intercession within us. The reason most of us are unable to intercede is because we have been building tents in the arena of hurt and disappointment. We must be willing to dismantle our tents and buildings in the wilderness of hurt and disappointment. Most of us don't want to let go. If we don't learn to sincerely release our pain, we will not be able to have a roadway to understanding that individual. That is why we react like we do.

4) It will cause in us a strong determination to seek reconciliation and even bless them sincerely.

Because you gave them the benefit of the doubt, you have simply transferred the blame from them to the devil. That enables you to bless them.

5) It would also help you to know how to properly relate to the individual who has hurt you, especially when you come in contact with them.

What this does is help you to understand the weakness and the problem of the individual. You then have the opportunity to strategize carefully in relating to them the next time.

What therefore is the principle of "The Benefit of the Doubt?" It is the process of ascribing or the transference of a person's mistakes, faults, attitudes or behavior whether good or bad, not to them, but to other circumstances around them and within them. It might be their age, their temper or their lack of understanding. It is simply the act of avenging evil with good. Every time you walk in this principle, you always look for the good in people. Let's look at a couple of examples.

If you were to call your friend a couple of times and you want to talk to them urgently because of an emergency you are going through and you are unable to contact them, there is a tendency that there would be a couple of thoughts that may come across your mind. You might be upset that they don't want to talk to you and thereby you'll make a decision never to call them again. All you need to do in this situation is to simply apply the "benefit of the doubt" principle and that is to ascribe that action of your friend to "Maybe he or she might have been busy," or "Maybe he or she was out or maybe nobody gave him or her your message." When you operate and apply this principle, it will give you the room to stay out of anger so that when you actually find out the reason, you will not feel that you have made a fool of yourself.

Let's look at another example. Say you greet an individual while they were talking to somebody else and they did not respond to you. Instead of getting upset and leaving the environment mad or leaving with the feeling that they did not want to talk to you or that they are giving you the cold shoulder or that they are proud, or that they don't love you, the "benefit of the doubt" principle will say, "Maybe they did not hear you when you greeted them, or maybe they were very engulfed in the conversation and they did not hear you". Don't leave mad bearing a grudge or having bitterness the next time you see them. All too often, people have come to a wrong judgement of which they later regretted.

Say for example, we are always giving to someone and they don't seem to be giving back to you. Our first reaction would be to stop giving to that individual or to think that the individual is trying to take advantage of us. We may even think that the individual is very stingy. That may be true and also may not be true. But the principle of the "benefit of the doubt" would say in such an instance: "Maybe they don't have the money to buy me things or to give me things or maybe they don't earn a lot." Instead of going through the hurt, resentment and bitterness, the benefit of the doubt principle keeps you free from these spirits.

What if your child had a problem or a fight with another child in school or in your neighborhood and your child comes home with a bloody nose? The parent's first reaction would be to go straight to the school and either attack the child that hurt your child or to sue their parents or the school for allowing your child to be hurt. These are normally our first instincts. The "benefit of the doubt" principle sees it differently. It says "Maybe your child cursed them first or maybe your child did something to provoke the other child." Your child may not have done anything wrong. But operating on this principle will keep you from irrational actions. It will prevent you from being rash and hasty in your decisions. It will temper your hurt and keep you from becoming bitter and resentful.

THE JESUS EPISODE

And there were also two other, malefactors, led with him to be put to death.

And when they were come to the place, which is called Calvary, there they crucified him, and the malefactors, one on the right hand, and the other on the left.

Then said Jesus, Father, forgive them; for they know not what they do. And they parted his raiment, and cast lots.

Luke 23:32-34

Jesus Himself operated in this principle. Right on the cross of Calvary, He spoke, "Father, forgive them." Forgive who? Forgive those that hurt Him, lied on Him, misunderstood Him, misjudged Him, despitefully used Him; forgive those that betrayed His trust, and forgive those that crucified Him. He forgave those that spat on Him. He forgave those that whipped Him. He forgave those that stripped Him naked and gambled over His clothes. Jesus prayed to the Father to forgive His enemies. Imagine if you and I were in the same spot that Jesus was. We sure would have been resentful, bitter and we would have felt hurt, anguished and disappointed. We probably would have had a strong desire to exact revenge, especially towards someone like Judas who walked and ate with Him yet decided to betray Him.

But Jesus operated in the "benefit of the doubt" principle. He said "Forgive them, for they know not what they do." The "benefit of the doubt" principle says "They know not what they do." Jesus decided to ascribe their actions and mistakes to their ignorance of Him or to their lack of understanding of the things of God. Understanding this made it easier for Jesus to be able to endure the intense persecution and the agony of crucifixion. We might say, "Wait a minute... they knew what they were doing. They were adults and so they should be responsible for their actions." And that may be true, but Jesus saw it in a different way. He chose to walk in the principles of God and He chose to forgive. He knew the "benefit of the doubt" principle. Jesus still continues to operate this principle on our behalf. Most of us do not deserve what we have received. But the reason we are receiving the favor we receive is simply because of what the Blood has done for us.

THE JOSEPH EPISODE

Then Joseph could not refrain himself before all them that stood by him; and he cried, Cause every man to go out from me. And there stood no man with him, while Joseph made himself known unto his brethren.

And he wept aloud: and the Egyptians and the house of Pharaoh heard.

And Joseph said unto his brethren, I *am* Joseph; doth my father yet live? And his brethren could not answer him; for they were troubled at his presence.

And Joseph said unto his brethren, Come near to me, I pray you. And they came near. And he said, I *am* Joseph your brother, whom ye sold into Egypt.

Now therefore be not grieved, nor angry with yourselves, that ye sold me hither: for God did send me before you to preserve life.

For these two years *hath* the famine *been* in the land: and yet *there are* five years, in the which *there shall* neither *be* earing nor harvest.

And God sent me before you to preserve you a posterity in the earth, and to save your lives by a great deliverance.

So now *it was* not you *that* sent me hither, but God: and he hath made me a father to Pharaoh, and lord of all his house, and a ruler throughout all the land of Egypt.

Moreover he kissed all his brethren, and wept upon them: and after that his brethren talked with him.

Genesis 45:1-8,15

Let's see this principle in operation in the life of Joseph. If there is anyone that had just cause and reason to be mad, hurt, bitter and resentful, it was Joseph. He went through trials and persecutions from his own brothers. One can understand if the trials and persecutions came from an outsider or from a stranger. But it is much more painful when it comes from the one who is supposed to be your friend, your relative or a loved one. Joseph was in this exact predicament. He was taunted by his brothers because of his dreams. He was thrown into the pit to die. He was sold as a slave to the Ishmaelites, sold into Egypt, falsely accused of sleeping with the king's wife, and unjustly imprisoned. Joseph literally went through hell just because of the actions of a bunch of jealous brothers. But I want you to see his action and reaction when the opportunity came for him to take his revenge. I guess if we were in Joseph's shoes, we would be very bitter towards the brothers and resentful towards them. We might even ask for them to be thrown in prison. We would literally pay back what was done to us.

But Joseph took a different posture. He refused to be bitter and resentful. He refused to remain hurt. He refused to take revenge upon his brothers.

Instead, Joseph saw something much better than
bitterness. He saw something much greater than
resentment and unforgiveness. He saw the Hand of
God orchestrating the entire process from the very
beginning to where he was. He understood the path to
his destiny.

> **Then Joseph could not refrain himself before all them
> that stood by him; and he cried, Cause every man to
> go out from me. And there stood no man with him,
> while Joseph made himself known unto his brethren.**

> **And Joseph said unto his brethren, I *am* Joseph; doth
> my father yet live? And his brethren could not answer
> him; for they were troubled at his presence.**

> **Genesis 45:1,3**

The Bible says that Joseph could no more
refrain himself before his brothers. He wept in their
presence. Not because he felt bad for what they did
to him, but because of his love towards them. He was
happy to see them. That sounds opposite to what
most of us would do. Joseph walked in the "benefit of
the doubt" principle. The Bible says that the brothers
could not answer him when he finally revealed his
identity to them. I guess they wished the ground would
open up and swallow them. They must have felt guilty
and repentant over what they did to Joseph. Joseph's
approach was the approach of a man who knew God
and walked in the "benefit of the doubt" principle.

> **Now therefore be not grieved, nor angry with
> yourselves, that ye sold me hither: for God did send
> me before you to preserve life.**

For these two years *hath* the famine *been* in the land: and yet *there are* five years, in the which *there shall* neither *be* earing nor harvest. -

And God sent me before you to preserve you a posterity in the earth, and to save your lives by a great deliverance.

So now *it was* not you *that* sent me hither, but God: and he hath made me a father to Pharaoh, and lord of all his house, and a ruler throughout all the land of Egypt.

Genesis 45:5-8

He told his brothers, "Be not angry with yourselves, that ye sold me." They must have been overwhelmed with shame and remorse. The next thing he said was evidence of the "benefit of the doubt" principle in action: "For God did send me before you to preserve you a posterity in the earth and to save your lives by a great deliverance." Joseph began to ascribe the blame on God. He began to transfer their actions to be God -- orchestrated by His Hand. As long as he knew this, he was unable to be bitter towards his brothers. He saw something else in all of the problems, trials and difficulties and that thing he saw kept him going. Bitterness, unforgiveness and hurt could not grab hold of his mind, because he knew the cause of his brother's actions. When we come to this point in our walk with the Lord, it will become much easier to destroy and uproot every spirit of hurt, bitterness and resentment that the enemy might want to bring across our way.

CHAPTER FIVE

THE ATTITUDE OF FORTITUDE

Because of our wrong attitudes towards hurt, resentment, bitterness and unforgiveness, it has become very difficult for us to give forgiveness and let go of the portion of these attitudes that are lodged inside of us. We must have the right attitude towards hurt. We must nurture the attitude of fortitude, which will patiently and courageously confront the pain of conflict to bring resolution. I want you to see an example of someone in the Bible who at the beginning had a wrong response and attitude towards her hurt and bitterness. But later, she found out that she could not change anything with her attitude and could not receive what she wanted. She ended up changing her attitude and it was only at that point that God started blessing her. The way she reacted is exactly how most of us react when someone offends us or when we are hurt or in bitterness and resentment.

LEAH'S PAIN

And Laban had two daughters: the name of the elder *was* Leah, and the name of the younger *was* Rachel.

Leah *was* tender eyed; but Rachel was beautiful and well favoured.

And Jacob loved Rachel; and said, I will serve thee seven years for Rachel thy younger daughter.

And Laban said, *It is* better that I give her to thee, than that I should give her to another man: abide with me.

And Jacob served seven years for Rachel; and they seemed unto him *but* a few days, for the love he had to her.

Genesis 29:16-20

First of all, let's look at the scenario that caused Leah to develop this attitude of her hurt and bitterness. Leah was a despised wife of Jacob. Jacob really did not love her. The Bible says that she was just "tendered-eyed" and that Rachel was beautiful and well favored". She was a wife forced upon Jacob by Laban. Can you imagine being married to someone that really does not love you or care about you, but just tolerates you because they want your sister? To make it worse; not just your sister, but your "younger" sister? The sister whose diapers you changed, you bathed, you walked to school? Can you imagine that the sister you literally raised is the one that your husband now prefers more than you? That is a level of rejection that can be very devastating and hurtful.

A REJECTED AND SCORNED WOMAN

And it came to pass in the evening, that he took Leah his daughter, and brought her to him; and he went in unto her.

And Laban gave unto his daughter Leah Zilpah his maid *for* an handmaid.

And it came to pass, that in the morning, behold, it *was* Leah: and he said to Laban, What *is* this thou

hast done unto me? did not I serve with thee for Rachel? wherefore then hast thou beguiled me?

And Laban said, It must not be so done in our country, to give the younger before the firstborn.

Fulfil her week, and we will give thee this also for the service which thou shalt serve with me yet seven other years.

And Jacob did so, and fulfilled her week: and he gave him Rachel his daughter to wife also.

Genesis 29:23-28

And if that was not enough, she was a rejected and a scorned wife. Jacob was very unhappy and upset when he found out that it was Leah that he slept with. He did not like her. He was pretty angry. This can be very painful. To hear your husband telling your father that you were not the one he wanted after stealing your virginity can be very hurtful. Jacob preferred spending all his time with Rachel and not with her. She was not Jacob's first choice. No woman likes to be number two or second choice in the eyes of their husband. But that was Leah's situation.

THE HONEYMOON THAT TURNED SOUR

And it came to pass in the evening, that he took Leah his daughter, and brought her to him; and he went in unto her.

And Laban gave unto his daughter Leah Zilpah his maid *for* an handmaid.

And it came to pass, that in the morning, behold, it
***was* Leah: and he said to Laban, What *is* this thou**
hast done unto me? did not I serve with thee for
Rachel? wherefore then hast thou beguiled me?

Genesis 29:23-25

Leah must have anticipated a joyful, interesting
and romantic time on her honeymoon. But the moon
was not honey that day. Instead it was full of
bitterness, hurt and resentment. Jacob woke up the
next day and realized that the woman he slept with
was Leah and not Rachel. He was upset and with his
uncle Laban. Leah, like every other woman expecting
to lay on the chest of her husband and enjoy her
honeymoon, had a rude awakening. She found out
that she was just a mistake and that she was not the
one that her husband really loved. Imagine how
shattering this can be -- you loving someone and they
never reciprocate that love.

And Laban said, It must not be so done in our
country, to give the younger before the firstborn.
Fulfil her week, and we will give thee this also for the
service which thou shalt serve with me yet seven
other years.

And Jacob did so, and fulfilled her week: and he gave
him Rachel his daughter to wife also.

Genesis 29:26-28

To make it worse, after all of these experiences,
Jacob continued to use all of his energy, all his money
and all his available resources in working so as to

secure the love of his life -- Rachel. Seven years being married to Leah was concentrated in wooing, dining, dating and buying expensive gifts and presents for another woman -- Rachel, thereby torturing Leah every night by not showing her the true affection that she needed or deserved as a wife. He was spending his attention and money on the OTHER WOMAN. Leah's needs were not being met, simply because the husband who was suppose to meet that need was channelling and showering all his affection on a younger woman - her sister. You can just imagine, Leah being married and sleeping with a man that does not really love her, but instead loves somebody else. Imagine Jacob sleeping with Leah and calling Rachel's name. Imagine the thoughts that went on in Jacob's mind every time he was with Leah -- the thought of the younger, beautiful and well-favored woman, Rachel.

Let's try to bring this story home for a few minutes. Try to feel exactly what Leah must have been going through and if the same thing were happening to us today, how we would handle it or react to it.

The first reaction would probably be to feel extremely bitter against Jacob. Today, Jacob would be called various nasty names and Leah would be encouraged to throw him out and find another man who can love her, take care of her needs and appreciate her beauty. Or, some people would have strongly encouraged her to see the psychiatrist for marriage counseling. Or, she may have attempted to commit suicide. Or, she might even have sought a divorce.

Leah would probably become subject to a feeling of low self esteem. You will think that it was because you are not beautiful enough, not thin enough, not fat enough, that you don't have the proper build and shape, that your nose is too small or too big, too straight or too wide. That you are too dark skinned or light skinned and that you are too tall or too short. You might also resent Jacob and Rachel strongly and may never want to talk to your baby sister. You might also try to look for a good opportunity to revenge and retaliate against Jacob and Rachel to let them know that you are somebody. These are normally some of the many things we may decide to do, because we are hurt, bitter and resentful.

LOOK AT ME

And Leah conceived, and bare a son, and she called his name Reuben: for she said, Surely the LORD hath looked upon my affliction; now therefore my husband will love me.

Genesis 29:32

With these strong feelings of resentment, Leah's first reactions were the wrong responses. Leah probably reacted and responded to her hurt and bitterness just like most of us would react if we were in such a quandary of emotional disarray. It was after she tried the first reactions and found that they did not work, that she changed her attitude and response and began to deal with her hurt and bitterness God's way.

The first way Leah reacted and responded to her hurt was exactly the same way most of us react to hurt today. Leah's reaction and response was "LOOK AT ME." She gave birth to a son which she named "Reuben" and this symbolically speaks of her state and her posture of reaction. "Reuben" means "Behold a son." Leah thought with the birth of Reuben, Jacob would turn his total attention on her. That he would start now looking at her instead of Rachel. That is the first wrong way that we always react whenever we are hurt, offended and in bitterness. We always want people to look at our wounds, to look at our hurt, to look at what has been done to us, to look at how someone reacted to us. We crave for the attention. We want someone to pay us attention, to sympathize with us and when we don't get this, it gets us upset and bitter the more.

That is exactly what Leah was trying to do. She had a wrong attitude towards her hurt, towards her bitterness, and towards her resentment. She wanted to get the undivided attention of Jacob, her husband. She thought that if she could only have the child which means "Look at me" that she would be able to receive the love of Jacob. She thought that by producing a son, she would win her husband's approval. Having a child will never solve the problem of rejection.

HEAR US

And she conceived again, and bare a son; and said, Because the LORD hath heard that I *was* hated, he hath therefore given me this *son* also: and she called his name Simeon.

Genesis 29:33

53

The second way that we tend to respond and react to bitterness and hurt is that we always want people to "HEAR US". Whenever we get hurt, or someone offends us or in bitterness, we always want to seek out people who can hear us. Suppose you are in a gathering and somebody hurt you or offended you. The first thing you may want to do is to tell your friends or your phone buddy about what was done to you, and discuss whether you were right or wrong. We always like to seek out people who can hear us. Someone who can be a dust pan or a garbage bag for our hurt and bitterness. But God has already made Himself available. Instead, we prefer someone else. We crave a supporting cast. We don't want to feel like we are totally wrong. And if we can have a supporting cast that sees it the way we see it, it gives us a great deal of relief and gives us a sense of justification -- that is we are right and not wrong.

Secondly, we always want someone who can understand our view point, even though our view points may be wrong.

Finally, we always seek out a defense for our action. If we don't have one, we will feel like a fool.

Avoiding a supporting cast or supporting pool causes you to move into the arena of self-examination. You will have to examine yourself with the Word of God to see if your actions were right or not. Whatever decision you come to, you will have to move to the next step. A true spirit of repentance would be produced in you when you realize that you were wrong and acted stupid. You will desire to quickly ask God for forgiveness and start all over again on a new slate.

It would also produce growth in you. You will begin to mature in the things of God like you should. Things that used to irritate you will no longer affect you. As long as you continue to seek the pool of a supporting cast to vindicate what you are doing, you will never experience growth. You might think that you are growing, but the only thing growing in you is the number of years you are spending as a bitter, frustrated and hurting Christian.

And she conceived again, and bare a son; and said, Now this time will my husband be joined unto me, because I have born him three sons: therefore was his name called Levi.

Genesis 29:34

Often, we want to look for someone or something to which we can join or connect ourselves instead of us taking the opportunity to go back to Father so that He can pour the Balm of Gilead on our wounds and hurts. We turn to something else. We want to look for someone that is going through some kind of bitterness, resentment and forgiveness with which we can identify. We want some resentful cliques to create a "pity party" club, a "gossiping" salon and a "complaining and griping" forum. Many times we end up bonding to foods, alcohol, sex, drugs, television and shopping. None of these can offer a permanent remedy. Because of the bonding or connection to these things and more, we begin to see ourselves deeper into the camp of the enemy. We then develop obesity, bad sexual habits and become addicted to drugs.

Many also end up bonding with the wrong men and women. Leah thought that if she gave birth to "LEVI" which means "joined to", she would be able to resolve the hurt and the bitterness in her life. She thought that "LEVI" would make Jacob love and cherish her. LEVI speaks to us today of our state and position in responding to our hurts, our bitterness, our resentment and our unforgiveness. How do you respond to your hurt and bitterness? Do you look to be connected and bonded to people who will uphold your nasty attitudes when you're hurting? Or do you instead connect yourself to the Healer of all hurt -- Jesus Christ? What we ought to do every time we feel hurt or bitter towards a person or a thing is to run straight to our closet and allow the Spirit of God to pour a warm healing on our emotions. We should make the quality decision immediately to let it go.

JUDAH - THE RIGHT RESPONSE TO HURT, BITTERNESS, AND RESENTMENT

And she conceived again, and bare a son: and she said, Now will I praise the LORD: therefore she called his name Judah; and left bearing.

Genesis 29:35

The Bible says that Leah conceived again and bore a son and this time she decided to call him "JUDAH" meaning "PRAISE" or "I will praise the Lord". I guess we can say that Leah had to learn the hard way. Judah was the original place that God had ordained for Leah to visit with her hurts and bitterness. And Judah is still the place that God has ordained for us to visit today with our unforgiveness, hurt and bitterness. Just like Leah, many of us like to go around the wilderness hoping that a change would take place immediately. We love short-cuts. But the good news is that there are no short-cuts in God! You can either make up your mind to be permanently healed of your wounds and hurts by the Spirit of God or be temporarily healed by the psychiatrist.

Leah woke up and smelled the coffee! She actually realized that there was nothing she could do in her own strength to make her husband love her. She realized that she had her attention on the wrong person. She found out that the therapist could not give her the healing she needed. She finally turned her attention to the Lord. We need to learn from this story. There are many of us that are still using the wrong medicine to heal the wounds and hurts of our emotions. That new dress, that new home or even that new car cannot heal that hurt. Marrying that man or woman cannot heal you. Even relocating to a new state, new city or new church will not produce the true healing that you need. The true and permanent healing comes from the very bosom of the Holy Spirit. There are sufficient medicines made available for your kind of pain and hurt in the medicine cabinet of Heaven.

The right way to react and respond to our hurts, pains and unforgiveness is to go to JUDAH. Stay in Judah until you receive your victory. Judah speaks of praise, but it means more than just praise. Judah is supposed to be the origin of the Deliverer. The Deliverer is Jesus Christ. So that means that if the Deliverer will come from Judah, our deliverance will also come from Judah -- the place of the Deliverer.

PAUL AND SILAS' EXPERIENCE IN JUDAH

And it came to pass, as we went to prayer, a certain damsel possessed with a spirit of divination met us, which brought her masters much gain by soothsaying:

The same followed Paul and us, and cried, saying, These men are the servants of the most high God, which show unto us the way of salvation.

And this did she many days. But Paul, being grieved, turned and said to the spirit, I command thee in the name of Jesus Christ to come out of her. And he came out the same hour.

And when her masters saw that the hope of their gains was gone, they caught Paul and Silas, and drew *them* into the marketplace unto the rulers,

Who, having received such a charge, thrust them into the inner prison, and made their feet fast in the stocks.

And at midnight Paul and Silas prayed, and sang praises unto God: and the prisoners heard them.

And suddenly there was a great earthquake, so that the foundations of the prison were shaken: and immediately all the doors were opened, and every one's bands were loosed.

And the keeper of the prison awaking out of his sleep, and seeing the prison doors open, he drew out his sword, and would have killed himself, supposing that the prisoners had been fled.

But Paul cried with a loud voice, saying, Do thyself no harm: for we are all here.

Then he called for a light, and sprang in, and came trembling, and fell down before Paul and Silas,

And brought them out, and said, Sirs, what must I do to be saved?

And they said, Believe on the Lord Jesus Christ, and thou shalt be saved, and thy house.

Acts 16:16-19, 24-31

Paul and Silas were examples of men who took advantage of the available healing in Judah. They were wrongfully accused of what they did not do. They were beaten and then thrown into prison. They probably had all the reason on earth to resent the people that did this to them and become bitter at God. They had served the people through preaching and working miracles, and were imprisoned for their efforts. They had left all to follow Christ and had been faithful to preach the Gospel. They were obedient, so why should they be in prison? They could have been mighty bitter. But the Bible says, instead of Paul and Silas taking the routes discussed earlier, they went straight to Judah -- the place of praise and deliverance. The Bible says that they "sang praises." That sounds stupid and crazy, right? You say "How can I sing praise to God when I am hurt?" "How can I sing praise to God when I was abused by my father, my husband, and my mother?" "How can I sing praise to God when I was raped or when my friends lied on me?" "How can I sing praise in the midst of a divorce?" Paul and Silas could have wallowed in self-pity the same way. But they chose not to take this route. Instead, these two folks turned to Judah. I am not saying that there won't be pains. But always remember that every pain is just an alarm clock to let you know that your baby - the healing, the vision -- is about to be birthed! When you enter the realm of Judah, you may be in pain. But don't give up and go back! It is not wrong or sinful to be knocked down. But it is wrong to be knocked out! So stay and overcome the pain in Judah! The Bible says that as Paul and Silas began to praise God, the prisoners -- the enemies heard them "and suddenly there was a great earthquake". Many of us stop our praise when we don't feel anything. We stop our praises when we don't feel the goose bumps. We must praise God until the prisoners of our emotions, of our hurts, our bitterness and our resentment hears us. Whether we feel like it or not. You may ask how far do you need to go in your praise? Until your prisoners hear you. How do your prisoners hear you? When you begin to sense a release in you and begin to feel a note of victory dropped in your spirit, for it is only at the point where the prisoners of our hurts, of our emotions and of our wounds hear us that there can be a "great earthquake" that would shake the very foundation of that hurt, of that wound, of that bitterness and of that unforgiveness.

And when this happens, the closed door of our hurts and bitterness would be broken open by the power of God and every chain of unforgiveness would be loosened. Then our lives would become lives of testimony and deliverance to people who have not known the power of God. The Bible says that not only were Paul and Silas loosed from their bands, but the keeper of the prison was also released from his bands. You cannot afford to loose anyone unless you have first been loosed by the power of God. For us to be vessels that God uses to release people from prison, we must make sure that we are not in prison ourselves.

CHAPTER SIX

THE POWER OF FORGETTING

It is not conceited - arrogant and inflated with pride; it is not rude (unmannerly), and does not act unbecomingly. Love [God's love in us] does not insist on its own rights or its own way, for it is not self-seeking; it is not touchy or fretful or resentful; it takes no account of the evil done to it - pays no attention to a suffered wrong.

It does not rejoice at injustice and unrighteousness, but rejoices when right and truth prevail.

1 Corinthians 13:5-6 (Amp)

I, even I, am He Who blots out and cancels your transgressions for My own sake, and I will not remember your sins.

Put Me in rememberance - remind Me of your merits; let us plead and argue together. Set forth your case that you may be justified - proved in the right.

Isaiah 43:25-26 (Amp)

Forgiving and forgetting go together. God's says that He forgives us of our sins and puts them as far as the east is from the west and remembers them no more. A lot of times, we try to forgive people and continue to remember what they did to us. Most Christians are the best accountants available. They are good in taking account of the evil that was done to them. And often when most Christians are asked about the need to forgive, many Christians wonder who they should forgive. They say "I didn't do anything wrong to him" or "I don't even know who to forgive."

We need to forgive those who have hurt us. Whether they are close to us or not, and whether we like them or not. We need to forgive people that hurt us a long time ago. We need to also forgive people on a daily basis. Forgiveness needs to be a lifestyle. Unforgiveness is considered to be one of the power demons. It is not a little problem. It is a big problem.

FORGIVE YOURSELF

Not that I have attained [this ideal] or am already made perfect, but I press on to lay hold of (grasp) *and* make my own, that for which Christ Jesus, the Messiah, has laid hold of me *and* made me his own.

I do not consider, brethren, that I have captured *and* made it my own [yet]; but one thing I do - it is my one aspiration: forgetting what lies behind and straining forward to what lies ahead,

I press on toward the goal to win the [supreme and heavenly] prize to which God in Christ Jesus is calling us upward.

So let those [of us] who are spiritually mature *and* full-grown have this mind *and* hold these convictions, and if in any respect you have a different attitude of mind, God will make that clear to you also.

Only let us hold true to what we have already attained *and* walk *and* order our lives by that.

Philippians 3:12-16 (Amp)

Be watchful, and strengthen the things which remain, that are ready to die: for I have not found thy works perfect before God.

Revelation 3:2

The next person you need to forgive is yourself. Sometimes, when we get involved in something terrible, we cry out to God to forgive us. When we cried out to Him, He forgave us. But we also need to forgive ourselves. God forgives us the first time we ask Him to. What we need to do is to receive that gift of forgiveness that God is trying to give us.

There are Christians who were once abused and perpetuate the abuse by abusing their children or someone else. They're finding it difficult to forgive themselves. Maybe you committed adultery, fornication or some little or serious sins and you immediately ask God for forgiveness. He has forgiven you. But you are still finding it difficult to forgive yourself. If you are in this situation or condition, you need to forgive yourself. Forgive yourself for the child you had out of wedlock. Forgive yourself for that mistake. No matter how terrible it is, forgive yourself. Maybe you once had an abortion and nobody knows, but you have asked God to forgive you. He did, but now you need to forgive yourself and not do it again. Maybe you have been in prostitution or have been in homosexuality and you have repented and turned your life over to Jesus. God forgave you. But yet you are still badgered by it. You need to forgive yourself.

You must forgive yourself so that you can receive those things you have been crying out for God to provide. The devil deceives you by telling you that you don't deserve the forgiveness from God and so he torments you with guilt which doesn't allow you to forgive yourself. Nobody deserves forgiveness. But God just gives it because He is our merciful and gracious Father. If we were all to get what we deserve, we'd all go to hell. We must realize that we are continually recipients of blessings that we don't deserve. Sometimes we get into the mentality that says, "God, if you are going to be this good and nice to me, I will receive what you have for me, but I have to work for it." But you don't have to work for it.

Some of us will not forgive ourselves because we feel that we have disappointed God. Many people go through this and think that they are being punished. You cannot go forward with God if you are going to hold against yourself the things that you have done in the past. If you are going to punish yourself afresh all the time for your past mistakes, you can't move forward in life. The only way you can go forward is to let go of what is behind you.

You cannot buy forgiveness by punishing yourself with self-rejection. You see, some people, because of their past mistakes and past sins and even things and situations that they are presently habitually having problems with, end up rejecting themselves. It's as if they don't like themselves. They just hate themselves. They end up with an inferiority complex about themselves, and dwell in a desert place.

TO THOSE WHO ARE THIRSTY

Wait *and* listen, every one who is thirsty! Come to the waters; and he who has no money, come, buy and eat! Yes, come, buy *priceless* [spiritual] wine and milk without money and without price [simply for the self-surrender that accepts the blessing].

Isaiah 55:1 (Amp)

This Scripture is worth rejoicing about! It says everyone that is THIRSTY. Are you in a desert place? Are you one of the thirsty? Those that are thirsty for forgiveness? Those who want to be free within themselves about their past mistakes? "He who has no money, come, buy and eat." This is talking about those of you who have no way to purchase what you need from God. You don't know how to go about remedying the situation. It says "without price". But then it says that the only requirement is total self-surrender. Why? Because it is the self-surrender that accepts the blessing. What is the price God wants? Just self-surrender. Just go to Him and throw yourself on His mercy. Your sacrifice is to stop fighting God. That is what He is saying. What is my big part? Just surrender and let God bless you and give you what you don't deserve. Humble yourself and quit trying to earn God's goodness!

The Spirit of the Lord God is upon me, because the Lord has anointed and qualified me to preach the Gospel of good tidings to the meek, the poor and afflicted; He has sent me to bind up and heal the brokenhearted, to proclaim liberty to the [physical

**and spiritual] captives, and the opening of the prison
and of the eyes to those who are bound**

Isaiah 61:1 (Amp)

Tell Him what He already knows. "I am a mess", "I am a cheat", or "I am a fornicator." Ask Him to forgive you for your sins, for your faults, for your shortcomings and for your slips and then by faith receive from Him forgiveness that you don't deserve. One of the benefits of the anointing is to bind up and heal the broken hearted. So whatever things that have happened in the past whether you were hurt, disappointed and cannot forgive yourself, the Bible says that the anointing is available to bind it up and to heal it. Take advantage of the anointing! The anointing is available for the opening of the prison and of the eyes to those who are bound. Do you know what this means? It means that the prison of unforgiveness has been opened and Jesus has the key! He wants to open our eyes to see that it has been opened.

A lot of Christians' prison doors have been opened for years and yet they have been sitting in the cell waiting for the door to open. In the spiritual realm, your prison door is already open. Now your part is to decide to walk out. Some Christians are addicted to being against themselves. People can become addicted to guilt and condemnation. They just have to keep on beating up on themselves. God has done His part. It is our job to take advantage of what He has done. We need to learn how to be good receivers.

FORGIVING GOD

Who shall separate us from the love of Christ? *shall* tribulation, or distress, or persecution, or famine, or nakedness, or peril, or sword?

As it is written, For thy sake we are killed all the day long; we are accounted as sheep for the slaughter.

Nay, in all these things we are more than conquerors through him that loved us.

For I am persuaded, that neither death, nor life, nor angels, nor principalities, nor powers, nor things present, nor things to come,

Nor height, nor depth, nor any other creature, shall be able to separate us from the love of God, which is in Christ Jesus our Lord.

Romans 8:35-39

Therefore seeing we have this ministry, as we have received mercy, we faint not;

We are troubled on every side, yet not distressed; *we are* perplexed, but not in despair;

Persecuted, but not forsaken; cast down, but not destroyed;

Always bearing about in the body the dying of the Lord Jesus, that the life also of Jesus might be made manifest in our body.

For all things *are* for your sakes, that the abundant graoe might through the thanksgiving of many redound to the glory of God.

For which cause we faint not; but though our outward man perish, yet the inward *man* is renewed day by day.

While we look not at the things which are seen, but at the things which are not seen: for the things which are seen *are* temporal; but the things which are not seen *are* eternal.

II Corinthians 4:1,8-10,15-16,18

The next person that you need to forgive is God. This might seem stupid to some Christians. But there are a lot of Christians that have unforgiveness towards God. Sometimes, when people have a lot of disappointment in their lives, it can cause a bitterness and a resentment towards God. We blame God. Sometimes you blame Him for the death of your son, daughter or your loved one or sometimes we blame God for not answering or doing that thing that we have been believing Him to do for years. Sometimes we blame God for not being there when our brother or sister was sick and died.

This has caused a lot of Christians to backslide and lose their confidence in God. Some may even feel that God is not real. Often we say "Where were You when I needed You?" It is a very dangerous place to be when you have unforgiveness and bitterness towards God. Forgive God if you are in this situation. One of the things you must believe if you want to remain successful and happy in God is that God is good, that He is just and that God is merciful and gracious. No matter what is going on in your life right now. No matter how bad and tough things are, don't

70

blame God. It is not God's fault. We may not always understand it, but I tell you, God is good, He is perfect, and He is right. And when there is fault and error, it is on the part of man or it is brought in by the devil and we need not to get into the attitude of blaming God.

The question now is, "Are you mad with God?" If you are, I am going to ask you today to give that up and say, "Lord, I forgive You." Rule number one is to drop it. You cannot forget it if you yourself are going to keep the thing stirred all the time. Just drop it. And interesting enough, that is the definition that the Amplified Bible gives to forgiveness -- leave it, let it go, and drop it. In other words, you can carry it or you can drop it. The decision is yours.

LEARNING TO FORGET

Forgiveness is not complete until you forget. There are many individuals who claim to have forgiven people and yet they have not forgotten the errors done to them. True forgiveness is accompanied with amnesia for the mistakes, the bitterness and resentment that were generated. God practices true forgiveness and as children of God, we must determine to walk in the forgiveness in which our Father walks. What does it mean then to forget?

The word "forget" means "unable to remember." That is just one part of it. But I don't think that is the case with forgiving and forgetting. God is not saying that we cannot remember, but instead He is encouraging us to choose not to remember. It is a choice. We are in control over what we think. It is a choice that we *have* to make.

The word "forget" also means "to neglect." In other words, that wound might still be there in your thinking, and you might still be able to drag it up and rehearse it over and over. But God says even though it is there, neglect it and act like you are not paying attention to it. Ignore it.

Another definition of the word "forget" means "to fail to mention." There are a lot of those old time wounds which we need to fail to mention, instead of going around with our accounting list.

The word "forget" also means "a lack of concern for" -- for what? For that thing that was done to you. In other words, I know that they did it to me, but I am not concerned about it. We need to know how to cast our aches, wounds and pains that have been inflicted upon us from way back to the present time and just simply say, "God, that is not my concern or my care and I cast that care over on You. I give it to You, God. It is in Your Hands and You take care of it and You pay my debt".

We cannot forgive if we cannot forget. So we can lie to ourselves and tell ourselves that we have forgiven him or her. Just simply because you came to the altar and claim that you want to forgive that individual or have forgiven that individual does not mean that you have forgotten about it. You have to work through the process of forgetting it and that is your choice. You have to do that. God will not do it for you. You cannot sit down and start meditating and feasting on what was done to you and yet you said you have forgotten.

You have to know that in the process of your making a concrete decision to forget a wrong or a thing done to you, the devil has a way of bringing people that will help you to remember it. Even your very best friend who loves you very much can be used by the enemy to remind you. You must be willing and able to stand boldly and make up your mind that you will not remember and accept it anymore.

Understand that the thing that has hurt us is back in our past. But yet we have the ability to take a trip and go and visit it anytime we like. Most of us do, because we missed it. The memory of a thing is etched in our brains, and we can always go back anytime we want to dig out that memory or to have a party with that memory. That is what the psychiatrist and psychologist often do. They help you take a trip to things which you have forgotten.

If you have passed by something in your life at one time that has devastated, wounded, or hurt you, why would you keep looking back to the thing and let it wound you afresh all over again? It is like self torture. Sometimes, we can live in the good things that God has done for our life too long. Not just the bad things, but the good things. Just like we must not dwell on the bad things too long, we must also learn not to dwell on the good things too long. It would make you complacent. Get ready for more, God has more good things to do for you. Being anxious for tomorrow only causes you to lose today. Remember that the hills that are removed will never remain mountains to climb.

CHAPTER SEVEN

THE WEAPON OF FORGIVENESS

And forgive us our debts, as we also have forgiven (left, remitted and let go the debts, and given up resentment against) our debtors.

Matthew 6:12 (AMP)

Forgiveness is a strong weapon and when we understand how awesome this weapon is in the hands of God, we will begin to see the need to forgive people in a different way. Forgiveness is not an act of weakness, but an act of strength that enables us to witness the very nature of God. Bitterness, on the other hand, clogs up the love of God within us. We must determine to rid ourselves of bitterness and walk in forgiveness with all mankind. God expects us to forgive the way we have been forgiven. How have we been forgiven? Completely! How are we to forgive? We are to forgive the same way.

Beloved, let us love one another; for love [springs] from God, and he who loves [his fellow men] is begotten (born) of God and is coming (progressively) to know *and* understand God-- to perceive and recognize and get a better and clearer knowledge of Him,

He who does not love has not become acquainted with God-- does not *and* never did know Him; for God is love.

I John 4:7-8 (AMP)

Ironically, there are only two times in the New Testament where the Bible mentions to love Jesus or to love God. However, there are over one hundred times when it says, "Love one another." The way we treat one another shows the Father what we really think about Him. It is important that we learn how to treat one another. We must be open and honest with one another and also we must know how to get along. I want you to notice something about this verse that is very important. The verse above looks harmless until you understand that the word LOVE is always *agape*, unconditional love. The world's best kind of love says, "I love you, if you love me." God's love says, "I love you even if you don't love me." That is what He requires us to use day by day to measure out to people, whether they are nice or ugly to us. It is time that we allow the Bible to dictate to us what is right, whether we know Jesus Christ personally in our life or not. It is important that we have the biblical fruit or the biblical evidence of salvation to know that we know in our hearts that Jesus is Lord of our lives. When you know Jesus, you cannot sin successfully. You can sin, but not successfully. If some reason you fall into a state or condition of unforgiveness with someone and remain in that condition year after year without feeling convicted, I declare to you what Paul said to the Church at Corinth, "examine yourself and see if you be in the FAITH."

[Dear] little children, I am to be with you only a little longer. You will look for Me and, as I told the Jews so I tell you now, you are not able to come where I am going.

John 13:35 (AMP)

The greatest strategy that the enemy is using against the Body of Christ today is the strategy of "divide and conquer." The enemy creeps into our lives and causes us to have an offense toward someone and that offense develops into full-blown unforgiveness, following a season of neglect. The devil then utilizes this unforgiveness to build and develop a strong foothold into our lives to defeat us any time he wants to. Instead of taking care of the situation, what we frequently do is blame the offense on somebody else. We say "Lord, they did it. I didn't do anything." What we must understand is that if we even take up the offense, we still open the door to the enemy. We might not be guilty of doing anything, but when we pick up the offense we have given the enemy a foothold in our lives. We must keep the doors closed and choose to love even when we are not loved.

There needs to come a new and healthy fear upon the Body of Christ for treating one another the correct way, so that we in turn keep the enemy out of our midst. There must arise a new understanding of unity and oneness in our being.

LOVE COVERS

The sons of Noah who went forth from the ark were Shem, Ham, and Japheth. Ham was the father of Canaan [born later].

These are the three sons of Noah, and from them the whole earth was overspread *and* stocked with inhabitants.

And Noah began to cultivate the ground, and he planted a vineyard;

And he drank of the wine, and became drunk; and he was uncovered *and* lay naked in his tent.

And Ham, the father of Canaan glanced *and saw* the nakedness of his father, and told his two brothers outside.

So Shem and Japheth took a garment, laid it upon the shoulders of both, and went backward and covered the nakedness of their father, and their faces were backward and they did not see their father's nakedness.

When Noah awoke from his wine, and knew the thing which his youngest son had done to him,

He exclaimed, Cursed be Canaan! He shall be the servant of servants to his brethren! [Deut. 27:16]

He also said, Blessed be the Lord, the God of Shem, *and* blessed by the Lord my God be Shem! And let Canaan be his servant.

May God enlarge Japheth, and let him dwell in the tents of Shem; and let Canaan be his servant.

And Noah lived after the flood 350 years.

Genesis 9:18-27 (AMP)

The enemy is constantly looking for a avenue to get to us. The Bible explains emphatically what love does. Love never exposes, but it covers. Love always covers. When people are ugly to you, love covers. Look at what happened to Noah. During his celebration following coming out of the ark, he got drunk and fell asleep in his tent naked. Ham, one of his sons, walked in and saw him naked and said, "My God! Look at dad's nakedness." He walked out and told his brothers about the ugly condition of their father, Noah. The two brothers heard the words spoken by Ham and they did not think that it was funny. They walked towards the tent and when they opened its door, the Bible says they turned around backwards, picked up a cloth and began to approach him in a way that they would not see his nakedness. They made a quality decision not to see it. The nakedness was there. It was real. Noah had blown it, but they chose not to witness it. Instead, they opted to cover his nakedness, his condition. The only problem for Ham was that God saw Ham's reaction and He cursed the descendants of Ham while He blessed the descendants of Shem and Japheth, Ham's brothers.

Our Father God is in the covering business. We, therefore, as His children, should not be in the exposing business. We must line ourselves up with the business of our Father which is to cover and not to expose. We must learn to deal with the sins of our brothers in the right way. We are a family. We are to be unconditionally loyal to one another. If there is a need for Church discipline, the Church's leadership is adequate. They are able to handle it. Allow them to deal with it.

CHICKENS VERSUS BLUE JAYS

There is a beautiful illustration that really brings clarity to what I have been saying here so far. The illustration includes chickens and blue jays. Picture an injured chicken inside a crib with other chickens around it. If the injured chicken has a wound or blood spots on its body, the surrounding chickens will proceed to peck him until he dies. They have no intention to assist in nursing the wounds, only destroying the wounded. This scenario is too often witnessed in Christendom. Many believers are wounded, hurt or fallen and what do we do? We begin to peck at the injured! How? By saying, "I can't believe that they did that," "they knew better than that," "I can't believe that they have fallen." There are a lot of us just like chickens, we peck away at the injured, wounded or fallen. There is no love, no covering taking place. We are guilty of just pecking away, exposing the hurts, injuries and wounds of others. We are not accustomed to nursing our fellow brother and sister back to the faith. We prefer to share the news as a form of treatment. Sharing one's hurts are okay if the motive behind it is adequate. Why are you sharing that one's hurts? Is it your intention to see that individual restored? Or, is it your hidden agenda to inflict the final blow in the life of that person?

Are you aware of what blue jays do if a baby blue jay falls out of its nest to the ground and you happen to be the unfortunate one that walks by. The other blue jays will risk their very lives and swoop down upon you and peck you to try to keep you away from that which is hurt and wounded. God help the Church to be more like blue jays than chickens. You see, if we transfer the attitudes of some Christians or some church folks to the blue jays, here is what they would do. When that one blue jay falls out of its nest, they would all swoop down on him and say, "You finally did it, didn't you." They would say, "Yes, we knew you would end up like this. You made up your own bed now. You are going to have to figure out how to get back to the nest yourself because we are not going to help you." God forbid!

Some of us don't even say that to our brothers and sisters. Instead, we just ignore them. Most people that are hurt and wounded would much rather you just say something to them. "Don't walk away from me. Cover me! Help me! I have been snared by the enemy. Please help me!" is the cry in the heart of the wounded in the Body of Christ. This must cease before we become strong and formidable. We must cover one another's wounds. We must see that each and every one of the wounded are correctly and completely nursed back to health before returning to the battlefield.

DISPERSING AND
REVERSING OFFENSES

Let's look at one important practical thing that we can do with an offense. In prior chapters of this book, we learned that we must not curse the situation when we are offended, that we must not nurse the offense and that we must not rehearse the offense. But there is a very important principle that I believe will produce deliverance in our lives when we begin to walk in it.

We must learn how to disperse the offense. When we are willing to disperse an offense, God in return, will reverse it for our good. God makes it clear to us that vengeance is His and He will repay. God is capable of repaying. What we are to do when we are offended is dispersed it to the Lord. We aren't to let it get stuck in us where we take up the offense. What we are to do is to say to God, "Father, I disperse this offense to you and I am believing You to repay me."

The devil brings an insult or injury our way to try to cause us to take up the offense so that he can find an inroad into our lives. What we must do is to choose not to take up an offense, but disperse it to God, causing it to backfire while He reverses it on the person.

And Stephen, full of faith and power, did great wonders and miracles among the people.

Then there arose certain of the synagogue, which is called *the synagogue* of the Libertines, and Cyrenians, and Alexandrians, and of them of Cilicia and of Asia, disputing with Stephen.

And they were not able to resist the wisdom and the spirit by which he spake.

Then they suborned men, which said, We have heard him speak blasphemous words against Moses, and *against* God;

And they stirred up the people, and the elders, and the scribes, and came upon *him*, and caught him, and brought *him* to the council,

And set up false witnesses, which said, This man ceaseth not to speak blasphemous words against this holy place, and the law;

For we have heard him say, that this Jesus of Nazareth shall destroy this place, and shall change the customs which Moses delivered us.

And all that sat in the council, looking stedfastly on him, saw his face as it had been the face of an angel.

Acts 6:8-15

When they heard these things, they were cut to the heart, and they gnashed on him with *their* teeth.

But he being full of the Holy Ghost, looked up stedfastly into heaven, and saw the glory of God, and Jesus standing on the right hand of God.

And said, Behold, I see the heavens opened, and the Son of man standing on the right hand of God.

And he kneeled down, and cried with a loud voice, Lord, lay not this sin to their charge. And when he had said this, he fell asleep.

Acts 7:54-56, 60

There was a man named Saul of Tarsus, a Pharisee, who was breathing threats while coming into Jerusalem to persecute the followers of the Way. When he came in, he stirred up a riot and finally they singled out one man, Stephen, a man full of faith and of the Holy Ghost, a deacon in the Church of Jesus Christ. Stephen preached one of the greatest messages recorded to mankind. After he got through his message, the Bible says that they took him to a stoning pit and there Saul of Tarsus, who was the initiator of the whole event, did not throw one stone. But instead he held their coats while they stoned and killed the man of God.

Saul of Tarsus looked like he was home free from the incident but he had one problem-- before Stephen died, he said, "Father, forgive them. They don't know what they are doing." What did Stephen do? Before he died, he made sure that he dispersed his offense. The next stop for Saul of Tarsus was Damascus. God reversed the offense that Stephen dispersed and Saul had a visitation that changed his life completely. Child of God, hear me. We don't know what our Father will do with insults and accusations, with offenses that come our way that we disperse back to Him. We have to learn not to take up offenses for our own personal lives. But more importantly, so that we can be able to forge a strategy, frustrate the enemy and begin to see people that insult us receive total deliverance in their lives.

CHAPTER EIGHT

ENTERING THE FREEDOM ZONE!!

The following key steps allow us to understand the process of receiving forgiveness, forgiving and forgetting.

The first step is to **DECIDE**. If you are going to forgive anyone, you have to come to a point of decision. You must *decide* that you really want to forgive that individual. Many times people say that they forgive or they want to forgive, but in actuality they have not yet decided to forgive. They want to still enjoy the grudge, the bitterness and the resentment. They want to hold it for a long time. Some people would say, "Please give me more time to think this over." Think what over? To think whether to drop it or let it go?

You see, God had already decided before the foundation of the earth that when you hurt Him with your sins, He would forgive you. He did not wait until you did something wrong to decide. But He already decided before we were even created. That is exactly what God expects from us. We must decide before we get hurt or have any bitterness to forgive and forget.

You need to realize that there will be some people in your life that you will need to forgive over and over and over. In other words, they will give you the frequent opportunity to practice forgiveness on them. You will have to use them as target practice. There are some people out there that you just need to forgive once because you'll never see them again. But there are some people that you will have to see everyday and every hour that you need to continually forgive over and over again.

The guy that almost runs you off the road or almost steps on your toes in the grocery store will probably be seen once in your lifetime. But your brothers, sisters, mother, father, husband, wife, your boss, your co-worker, your pastor, and your children will be seen very often and you must be ready to forgive them over and over again. Why? Because the people you love the most have the greatest ability to hurt you than people that don't mean that much to you. And, because their personalities may just happen to rub you the wrong way. You have to settle this fact in your mind that there are going to be many people in your life that will not be just like you. They may not have achieved the height that you have achieved, and you are going to have many opportunities to be offended by them. If you want to walk in forgiveness, you must be ready and willing to absolutely depend on the Holy Ghost.

Your emotions may continue to act up when you get around that person even after you have made a decision to forgive them. Your emotions are not you, but they are just a part of you. They are not the spiritual you that makes decisions. But they are a part of you that will try to dictate situations and get you to obey them. How many of us have sincerely gone to the altar and really sought forgiveness and after a while, when you see the individual, the old beast begins to rise up in you so fast that if you don't leave the room, you will want to smack them in their heads?

Many times when people truly forgive and this happens, they tend to come under guilt and condemnation. But just understand that your part is to make the decisions and to depend on God through His Spirit, and God's part is to heal your wounded emotions.

STOP REHEARSING THE OLD STORIES

Death and life *are* in the power of the tongue: and they that love it shall eat the fruit thereof.

Proverbs 18:21

But I say to you who are listening now to Me (in order to heed, make it a practice to) love your enemies; treat well (do good to, act nobly toward) those who detest you *and* pursue you with hatred.

Invoke blessings upon and pray for the happiness of those who curse you; implore God's blessing (favor) upon those who abuse you - who revile, reproach, disparage and high-handedly misuse you.

Luke 6:27-28 (Amp)

Curse not the king, no not in thy thought; and curse not the rich in thy bedchamber: for a bird of the air shall carry the voice, and that which hath wings shall tell the matter.

Ecclesiastes 10:20

Stop talking about the people that offended or hurt you. Instead, pray for your enemies. Sometimes we don't talk about people openly. But we do in our hearts and what we say in our hearts carries the same gravity as talking about them openly. When we keep on talking about people that have offended us, in a negative way, we are speaking death -- sickness, hurt, disaster to them and part of it also falls on us. Normally, when someone hurts us, the very least we want to get out of it is some pity. We at least want somebody to feel sorry for us and be on our side.

BLESSING YOUR ENEMIES

Bless them which persecute you: bless, and curse not.

Romans 12:14

One of the most extremely important things that you must learn to do is become subject to Romans 12. You must learn to bless your enemy and do not curse them. The word "BLESS" means "to speak well of" and also "to be empowered to prosper." A lot of times, when we think about blessing people, we think about giving them something. That can be a blessing to people. But if you study the word *"bless"* in the Greek, one of the major definitions means "to speak well of them."

You will be confronted with daily opportunities to speak blessing into the lives of people. You may encounter those that are the exact opposite of you in temperament and personality. People that are completely different from us have a tendency to hurt or rub us the wrong way. They make us mad. They irritate us. They don't do things the way we like. Yet we must still love and accept them in spite of our differences. You need to remember that.

If the spirit of the ruler rise up against thee, leave not thy place; for yielding pacifieth great offences.

Ecclesiastes 10:4

The next group of people that we will have opportunity to forgive are those that are in authority over us. Why? Because they are more likely to tell you to do something that you don't like or want to do. You have a place, and the person in authority has a place. As long as you are truly under authority, you will have several opportunities to forgive those in authority over you. Whenever authority rises up against us to bring us some correction and we get out of our place and begin to come back against them, the Bible says that we are making room now for great offense. Not small offense, but **great** offense. This is exactly how a lot of problems get started. What we need to do is to learn to allow God to be our defense and not attempt to become our own defense. Whenever you are trying to do things yourself, God is not obligated to help you. You can either be vindictive or God can be your vindicator.

CHAPTER NINE

HEALING THE WOUNDS OF OFFENSE

How do you know if you still have hurts, resentment and unforgiveness lodged within you? Many times we hear people who have been hurt and in bitterness say "I don't have anything against them." "I am not bitter with him or her." "I don't have unforgiveness in my heart towards him or her." Often half of these people still have bitterness and resentment lodged within them. This is why it is important to understand some of these symptoms. Understanding these symptoms prepares you in focusing your attack on areas that need healing.

One of the important ways to find out if you still have unforgiveness locked within you is when the same old reaction rises up in you when you see the one that hurt you or with whom you had a conflict. Normally, as long as we are not in the vicinity or in the environment of those that offended or hurt us, it is always easy to go around like everything is alright. We even tend to forget that we have unforgiveness in our heart. But often, when we come in contact with them that old beast of bitterness and resentment begins to rise up. Then all of a sudden, it dawns on us that we still have unforgiveness lodged in our heart for that individual.

Another symptom is the kind of statements and words that come out of our mouths whenever the person's name or things about the person are mentioned. Normally when we are hurt and walking in bitterness, the mentioning of the name of the individual who offended us or any credit given to the person that hurt us, tends to get us even more upset. We don't want to hear their name. We don't want any good thing said about them. And anytime we hear good things said about them, there is always that temptation to discredit what was said, and tarnish their character. We always want to let the individual praising them know that they are not as great as they portray themselves to be or we want to tell the individual how ugly and bad they are. Our choice of words about those who have hurt us are usually not complimentary.

The next symptom is the reactions of our heart. It is very important to always check the reactions of our hearts when we say we have forgiven. The question is, when the thoughts about the individual comes up in your heart, is it a hundred percent pure, true, honest and peaceful or does it get you upset and mad and provide flashbacks of the offensive moment in your mind? Even when they call you on the phone to talk to you, do you dread answering the phone? You must understand that when you fully forgive and forget, your mouth will indicate what your heart has agreed to. These symptoms point to the fact that we have not let go. Bitterness and unforgiveness must be destroyed from its root for it to die. You cannot just cover your hurt or resentment by moving to another city or another state. You cannot cover your unforgiveness by buying a new fur coat or some new suits. You cannot just cover your hurt by saying "I am going to stay away from them". The bitterness will still be there. We must be willing to decide that we are going to destroy these spirits of bitterness, resentment and unforgiveness over our lives and we must be willing to deal with it from the root. Until the root of the problem is destroyed, there is still life in the tree of bitterness within you.

The fruit of your vine should yield the peaceable fruit of the Spirit; love, joy, peace, long-suffering, gentleness, goodness, faith, meekness and temperance, against such there is no law. Unforgiveness is like a blight in your garden, it will cause your fruit to rot. Yet the power of forgiveness will cause you to empower your garden, and you will flourish as the planting of the Lord, whose leaf will not wither.

CHAPTER TEN

A PRAYER OF DELIVERANCE

"Father, in the Name of Jesus Christ, I ask you to release upon me the grace of God -- the divine ability to completely forgive others. Allow Your power and anointing to touch me from the crown of my head to the soles of my feet. Heal every wound, every hurt and every resentment that I may be harboring. Give me the grace to embrace your principles and give those that have despitefully used or abused me the "benefit of the doubt."

I will to have the character of Jesus Christ. I refuse to remain angry and offended at anyone. I will not look for others to reinforce my bitterness, but I will come to You, the Author and the Finisher of My faith, so that You and I may reason together, and I will choose to forgive and forget.

I break the power of anger that has created bondage in my life in the Name of Jesus. I break the powers of fear and doubt and relinquish judgment of others unto You. I will not seek to avenge hurt, but I know that vengeance is Yours and You will repay. I embrace the peace of God that surpasses my understanding, and I thank You that I walk in wholeness today.

Father, from this day forth, I declare that I will produce good fruit and blossom in Your Presence. I am Your child, and am beloved of You. I thank You that You always hear my prayers.   Amen."

Now begin to rejoice and walk in the power of forgiveness in Jesus' Name!